# Notes
### from the
# u n i v e r s e

# Notes
## from the
# universe

new
perspectives
from an
old friend

## Mike Dooley

TOTALLY UNIQUE THOUGHTS®

For Amanda

# Foreword

If I told you there've been no mistakes, that I understand every decision you've ever made, and that the challenges you've faced, you've faced for everyone, would you listen?

If I told you that what you dream of, I dream of for you, that the only things "meant to be" are what you decide upon, and that all that stands between you and the life of your dreams are the thoughts you choose to think, would you try to understand?

And if I told you that you are *never* alone, that there are angels who sing your name in praise, and that I couldn't possibly be any more proud of you than I already am, would you believe me?

Would you? Even if I pulled your leg, made you blush, and winked between my lines?

Then I shall...

# It's me, the Universe.

I've got good news and bad news.

The good news, is that you've passed the audition! Yee-haa! You've earned your wings! You're a certified, bona fide Being of Light, capable of transcending all fears and manifesting all dreams. From here on out, you have but to dwell upon what you want, and I must bring it forth.

The bad news, is that this message was supposed to reach you eons and eons ago.

Sorry.

# Do you have *any* idea...
of how powerful you REALLY are?

Do you have *any* idea
of how far your thoughts reach?

Do you have *any* idea
of how many lives you've already touched?

Do you have *any* idea
of how much you've already accomplished?

*Do you?*

# Ever wonder

how many angels you have?

All of them.

They insisted.

# Whether it's praise, love,
criticism, money, time, space, power, punishment, sorrow, laughter, care, pain, or pleasure... the more you give, the more you will receive.

# Today, *you are a magnet...*

for infinite abundance, divine intelligence, and
unlimited love.

Actually, this has always been true.

# Anyone watching you?

Good. This is a double-secret exercise.

Pretend you just received a phone call with wonderful, mind blowing, life changing news!

As you put down the receiver, your arms fly up over your head with joy. Pumping fists, then waving palms, like you just crossed a finish line before throngs of adoring fans. You cover your face with your hands trying to contain the euphoria, but it doesn't work, so you reach for the sky again while shaking your head in disbelief. You're grinning, crying, and just so happy!

Yes! Life is awesome, and you feel so grateful!!!!!!!!

Got it?

Now if someone catches you doing this, just tell 'em it was your pet psychic who called, and they'll forget everything they just saw.

The Universe xxoo

PS - Show me what you want to feel, create the feeling within yourself, and I'll then orchestrate the circumstances, however outlandish, that will help you feel it again, and again, and again.

# Turn the jungles

of time and space... into a patio garden... by
realizing that its many mysteries actually conspire
on your behalf.

# To better understand

who you really are, understand *why* you want
what you want, getting to the emotions you seek.

To go even deeper...
ask yourself why *you think* you can't feel
those now.

# Life is like a dance

and we're partners. Setbacks, delays and detours? Heck, they're just like some of the steps in the Mambo, Tango, and Cha-Cha. If you dissected the movements and saw them without regard to the rest of the dance, everyone would look like total dorks. But when you see the big picture... poetry in motion.

In life, setbacks, delays and detours are often just my way of "keeping" you for something way better. Don't let them discourage you, don't lose faith, *and whatever you do, don't stop dancing.*

Your most able choreographer,

The Universe

PS - You choose the dance, the ballroom, or disco, and let me write the steps. K?

# It's *not* hard.

Time and space are the *playground* of the Universe,
not the Harvard of the Universe.

Kindergarten dressed as paradise, at recess.

# Bogged down,

spinnin' your wheels, out of time, frustrated, stressin'? It's the details. You're messin' with the details, which is a 1,000,000 times worse than messin' with Texas.

Messin' with the details is like trying to play tennis with a golf club, like trying to cook with yesterday's hot stove, or trying to find meaningful new friends at the mall wearing a chicken suit.

Just get clear on your vision - the end result. Think, think and let go. Follow your impulses, do what you can, act as if, and know you've done your part.

The Universe is the detail Queen, a perfectionist extraordinaire. Delegate.

Brock? (chicken speak)

PS - Of course, there is a time and a place for chicken suits, just not in Texas.

PPS - Remember what was just said about the details.

# One of your greatest challenges

is realizing that the hurdles of Time and Space,
are simply reflections of imagined hurdles.

See no problems.

# Was it you?!

We have some new "help" here and our incoming correspondence has been kind of garbled.

Someone was thinking big, I mean really big, and now the entire Universe has been thrown into action, aligning players, circumstances and coincidences that will miraculously fall into just the right place at just the right time. It's changed everything, absolutely everything. The world will never be the same.

Actually, this happens with your every thought. But if it was you, did you mean joy when you said toy? Sounded like you wanted every toy? Either way, consider it done, just let us know.

Tallyho,

PS - What are you gonna do with a piece of earth? (Or did you mean "peace on..."?)

You *do* have time.

# Someone bugging you?

Nah, way too easy.

Just like happiness,
disappointment is an "inside" job.

# Can you keep a secret?

You know the space between you and all things, the void. Like right now, the space between you and this book.

That's where I hide... and watch.

Looking to see what your expectations are; of yourself, others, abundance, health, and happiness.

And from this space... as I catch your thoughts, hear your words, and see all you do, no matter where we are... I manifest the next moment in time.

Tallyho,

PS - If you reach out now, into this space, you can feel me. I'm here. It's true. You're never alone.

# All that you *must* do,
### you've already done.

# Pssst... It's me again...
## the Universe.

You deserve more, you know, *much more*.
And I just happen to have "some". Imagine.

Try this. STOP trying to predict, and therefore limit, where it's going to come from. Just know it's going to come, and let me figure out the rest.

Cool?

By the way, you rock.

Shhhhh...

# Do you realize,

that the Universe cannot have, do and be more...
unless you have, do and be more?

Want it all.

(As if you didn't.)

# It's easy to look around

at all the people who already have what you want, notice how they differ from you, and then think that they are the "kind of people" for whom having what you want, comes naturally. Whereas you are not, otherwise you'd have it too.

Very rational thinking, and a super way for non-adventurers to avoid responsibility, rest on the sidelines, and watch more TV.

Adventurers, on the other hand, understand that they are exactly the kind of people who should have the things they want, otherwise, they wouldn't be blessed with wanting them.

# Sure, there may be a lot
of "real estate" between here and where you
dream of being, but the road, if you notice,
happens to run straight through
the middle of paradise.

# Wouldn't you just know it?!

You go to earth for a little adventure, some fun and games, some learning and growing, and the next thing you know, you're trapped in a sea of illusions, trying to figure everything out with a little human brain, sweating the details, and desperately seeking approval and appreciation.

Sounds like reality TV.

Here's what you do... No, you don't vote everyone off. You just remember how things really work.

You remember that the thoughts you choose to focus on, from this day forward, will become the things and events of the rest of your life, no matter where you've been, no matter what anyone else says, and no matter how scary things may seem to be.

# Behold, a new day...

with rainbows, sunshine and blue skies. New players, rebounds, and recoveries. Abundance, health and harmony... just like you've been picturing them, right?

Right?!

Please tell me you've been picturing them!!

# You are "here" (your life now)

and you want to go "there" (your dreamed of life).
And because both are physical places, it would
*seem* that you must manipulate the physical world
to go from "here" to "there".

*Ah-ha! This* is the ultimate illusion.

Physical places are simply mirages, reflections, of
an inner world, the world of your thoughts. So to
get from "here" to "there" you must do your
manipulating *within*.

A thought worth dwelling on - brought to you by
your friend, the Universe.

# To find the shortest path

to any dream, work with ideas, not facts. Dwell upon the end result, not the how's. And rely upon the Universe, not yourself.

# Secret excerpt

from "Illumination for Dummies: Time~Space Edition". Now a Best Seller in dimensions far, far away...

"It's like, between every single second of the day, there's a pause. Life is suspended. Frozen and unfrozen. Imperceptible to the physical senses because these moments and non-moments are all strung together by your thoughts, beliefs and intents which span the gaps, creating a complete and seamless picture. It's even happening now, between every word you've just read.

"It's during these pauses that the future is forged. And just as all "things" flicker like a firefly, so does time, during which the Universe is busy at work, flying into action, moving mountains, plotting circumstances, and planning coincidences, unrestrained by the limits of material existence, including cause and effect. This is where the magic lies."

"Each succeeding physical moment then reflects the creations of the previous *non-physical moment*, dependent not upon what has existed in the physical, but upon the usually slow evolution of your beliefs, intents and expectations that carry through both realities.

(Are you sitting down?)

The past can even be rewritten and memories inserted, so that never a beat is missed. (Scratch "can even be", and use "are often". Just pacing you to ward off brain freeze.)

"Next time you want something, play off these pauses, not time and space. Don't look to the physical, look to the unseen. And dwell in the realm of infinite possibilities."

But you knew that.

Tallyho, ho, ho,


PS – It goes on to say that the evolution spoken of *need not be slow.*

# There is no greater weapon...
than kindness.

A smile, a compliment, encouragement and compassion belong in the arsenal of every Time~Space Adventurer.

Today, may you crush, kill, and destroy the fears you encounter, in others, and in yourself.

En Garde.

# The root of every "evil"

is looking to time and space for meaning, for
solutions, for identity; for friends, love, and
laughter; wealth, health, and harmony.

The source of all things - material things - is spirit,
which is molded by thought (yours), and then,
without judgment, impressed upon matter, before
your very eyes. Trying to get what you want, no
matter what it is, by looking to time and space
first, is like putting the cart before the horse, and
will leave you feeling powerless, heartbroken,
even sick.

And dear heart, this is the candy-coated
version of the truth.

Tallyho,

# Isn't it strange,

how once you set your "gaze" upon something or someone, you get to decide what you'll see; good, bad or ugly. Yet still, you think "it", or "they", has something to do with your feelings and moods?

Don't fight it.

# Behold, a Being of Light,

radiant, illuminated, and full of grace. Come to lift humanity higher into the light. All bow and sing praise... Agh! It's you! What are you doing back in time and space?

Ah-ha. I see. Pretending. Well that's perfectly understandable. We all need to pretend once in a while.

So how's it going?

Yes indeed, challenges. Part and parcel of any worthwhile adventure.

Tell me, there's a rumor that in time and space, the illusions are soooooo captivating, the coffee soooooo rich, and the chocolate soooooo dark, it's easy to forget you're just making it all up and that all you have to do to awaken, is pretend your way to wherever it is you'd like to go?

Cream and sugar?

# Always...

that which you most need, is already at hand.

It's simply your incessant searching and belief in its absence, that keeps it from view.

# When you get there,
wherever "there" is for you, probably nothing else
will matter more, than wanting to help others
achieve as you have.

Who will you first reach out to? What will you do
or say? How will you conduct yourself in public?
How will you show them what you see?

Better start practicing.

# The only difference

between a friend and a foe, is that *you've* decided,
where love can grow.

There isn't a soul on the planet,
who doesn't crave your approval.

# A question,
from your friend the Universe:

Just how much time do you spend thinking big? I mean really, really BIG?

Good, *very* good! Because that's exactly how much of "it" you're going to get!

What a coincidence.

# Your "challenges"

are simply the manifestation of your so-called
invisible, limiting beliefs.

Not so invisible after all, eh?

# Dearest Dear Heart,

I'm sorry to write you like this, but it's just not enough that you tell me you adore me. That you love my mysterious ways, and that you're brimming with excitement for the infinite possibilities that lay before us. It's simply not enough, not for me, and not for you. "Pumpkin" you must show me.

You must go out into the world and greet each day with faith that I am with you. Engage the magic. Stride confidently into your affairs expecting a miracle, and go boldly in the direction of your dreams.

Darling, it's time to ratchet things up a notch. Time to play too, to take everything less seriously, to get our "groove on", because there's simply nothing, nothing, nothing, that we cannot do together... though it's you, "sunshine", who must set us in motion.

Yours till the end of time,
The Universe

PS - You know, just do that thing you do, the one that drives me wild. Be all of you... and the rest will happen naturally.

Uga-chug-a, uga-chug-a, uga-chug-a.

# Do you realize,

that you have never heard anything, from anyone,
that you did not want to hear?

Pretty tricky of you.

# *Never* trust appearances.

# Just yesterday,

I was taking some time off, soaring through the sky, spread-eagle style, flying between some mammoth cumulus clouds, when BAM, I flew into a stork on a delivery run. Always loved storks, so simple, so accepting.

Felt bad for the poor fellow, so we flew together awhile and I chatted him up. I didn't tell him I was the Universe.

You know what he told me?

He said there are no accidents.

"None?" I asked, feigning surprise.

"None."

"Well then, it sure was a nice coincidence, running into you like this." And after sputtering a bit, he said there were none of those either.

"None?"

"Nope."

I asked him how he knew so much about life, being a stork and all. And he said there was a little bit of the divine in all of us; that we all know the truth about reality, and that by focusing on any problem or question, the answer is drawn to you.

"Get out of here." I told him.

"No, really, take today. I was wondering where all these babies came from, when BAM... suddenly, from nowhere, I just knew."

# Do you want to know

what the world starts looking like when you start
moving with an understanding that you are a
sublime Being of Light?

When you start realizing that you are the master
of your destiny?

Knowing that all things are possible, and that the
Universe does conspire tirelessly on your behalf?

Yeah, pretty much the way it looks right now.

# You simply have to change
your worldview - your opinions and beliefs - in
order to change your experience.

Tricky? Maybe.

Worth the effort? Depends.

How badly do you want greater peace of mind,
more friends and laughter, health and comfort, and
enough abundance to *never* have to
ask "how much"?

# It's not real! Don't go there!
The things *and events* of time and space are like
"play-doh"; fictional, make believe.

What matters are what you feel in your heart and
the dreams that flit through your head. This is the
ultimate test, to discover what's real in a
sea of illusions.

You *can* do it, or you wouldn't be here. Don't look
to the world for clues, not even to your family,
friends, or career. Look within. You decide what's
right. You decide what's possible. You write the
script and lay down the laws. *You* are the door, the
path, and the light.

# The things and events

of time and space... the stuff that's surrounding you now, your memory of recent events, all simply reveal where you've been, *not where you're headed.*

# Giving tells the Universe

that you believe *you* are provided for. For even as
you empty your purse you fear not, demonstrating
faith that you will remain whole, that your coffers
will be replenished, and that your love for
whomever you give, is what's most important.

Verily, as you believe these things to be true, you
will experience such truths, and abundance shall be
showered upon you as if the heavens had
opened up.

Adventurers 9:19

# Would a loving parent

ever give a child a story to read that didn't have a
wonderfully happy ending?

No. Never. But they might add, "Whatever you
do, don't stop reading at the scary parts!"

# Your invisible limiting beliefs

are only invisible when you live within their limits -
or when you keep on doing what you've always
been doing.

Push yourself. Dare yourself to think bigger, to
reach, and to behave as if a dream or two of yours
has *already* manifested. Then, you'll see 'dem little
buggers pop out of the woodwork painted
florescent orange, loaded to the teeth with logic,
imploring you to turn around and go back
to safety!

Do something, do it today, something you
wouldn't normally do. Like maybe... take off early
from work and go to a matinee movie.

Ahhh-ha! Did you just see a couple of 'em?!

Be warned, sometimes, once exposed, they'll try
to snuggle up to you, looking sooo innocent and
adorable. And as if that wasn't bad enough, they'll
start with their "baby talk". Sickening.

# Impatience is what you feel

when you think the future, in either hours, days, or years, will be "better" than the present.

It won't.

# If you only knew,

just how incredibly well everything is going to turn out, for you and those close to you, right now you'd likely feel light as a feather, free as the wind, happy, confident, giddy.

Whoops, kind of let the cat out of the bag there.

Well, now you know.

# I just had this extraordinary

conversation with one of your fellow adventurers, and I thought by sharing it, it might make a point or two:

Advanced soul: Dear Universe, I'm so grateful for all that I have, but life is hard and I don't know what to do.

The Universe: Precious Angel. Life is what you say it is, and you do know what to do.

Advanced soul: Thank you for hearing me and always tending to my needs, but I feel lost and confused.

The Universe: Dearest, I am with you, all day long I speak through your feelings and impulses. Go and be merry, but please, watch what you say and think. Refrain from stating that you are, what you don't want to be, "lost and confused".

Advanced soul: Aha! I feel you moving in me. I think I understand. All is well, together we move as one, but still, at times, I don't know if I'm on the right track.

The Universe: Radiant Child. Your future is certain, salvation is guaranteed, and all is well. You are adored, you are safe, and I have always been so proud of you. But if you keep saying you don't know, then you won't know.

Advanced soul: I know! I know! I am whole! I am complete! I know what to do! It's just that I also worry, my limiting beliefs are invisible, and life is hard.

Notice who gets the last word?

# When you look into the mirror

each morning, do you apply your make-up or shaving cream to your reflection in the glass?

Ha! Of course not, you'd be locked up. Instead, you go to the source of the reflection.

So then, when it comes to living the life of your dreams, the same philosophy should apply. Why try to manipulate the illusions of time and space, when you can go to their source, the inner world of your own thoughts, beliefs and expectations, where the real work is done anyway?

# Challenges in life

don't arise haphazardly, *no matter* how accidental
or coincidental they may seem. They only arrive
when *you're ready* for them.

Not when you're ready to be squashed, but when
you're ready to grow, overcome and be more than
who you were before they arrived.

# The reason that some

of your thoughts haven't yet become things... is because other thoughts of yours have.

# Adventurer Alert

Remember... You are an intergalactic, indestructible, unstoppable, eternal *Being of Light*, and for the time being, you're just pretending to be the little "hottie" holding this book.

K?

The Universe

# Ahhhhh, let's see here,

whose day shall I make? Whose week? Year? Entire life? Whose thoughts shall I endow with the power to become all things? Who will be made invincible to every challenge, and who shall I catapult over every obstacle? Who will get a second chance, a third chance? No, not enough, whose "life reset button" shall I hit whenever they want a "do-over"? Who will get their cake, and eat it too????

Oh, there I go again. Fantasizing, pretending, wishing it was really me who gets to decide such things, dang it. Wishing I could bestow such blessings, instead of just being the "techie" behind the scenes allowed to perform my miracles and magic only when called upon and believed in. It's like I'm life's Maytag repairman.

Use me. Please. So that I may fill your every cup, grant your every wish, and harvest your every dream. And let's begin today.

Guess I had to let that out.

Love you, whatever you choose,

The Universe

PS - It couldn't possibly be any easier than it is.

# The best way to deal
with other people... is to just let them be
other people.

After all, that's how you want them to deal
with you.

# Shhhhh....

The secret to living the life of your dreams,
is to start living the life of your dreams, *at once*,
to any degree that you possibly can.

# Just do it.

Everything you need to know, you know, and everything you need to have, you have. Everything!

Time and space is a primitive school. There are bigger challenges "out there", bigger adventures, and lots more friends, but you gotta do what you gotta do, here and now. You gotta live the truths you've discovered, apply the principles, and never again think, "Why isn't it working?", "It's hard.", "I don't know.", because such thoughts are like hitting the replay button for whatever you've just been through.

Look ahead with your dreams in mind and give thanks, because you know exactly what to do.

Phew... feel better?

Tallyho, ho, ho,

# As powerful as you are.....
## whose day are you going to make?

# What if you did have the power,

the reach and the glory? What if you were given dominion over all things? And what if eternity lay before you, brimming with love, friends and laughter?

Yet still, one day, in all your radiance, bubbling over with giddy excitement, you tripped, fell, and got hurt. Really, badly hurt.

Would you hate yourself? Would you give up on your dreams? Would you forget about your power, your reach, and the glory?

Oh, come now...

# Thinking...
## is the ultimate contact sport.

## All things considered...
you've never really asked for much.

Hey, what's up with that?

# Worldwide Proclamation!

This is to remind all my loyal subjects that you are not my loyal subjects. And that I'm bloody tired of all the sacrifices, appeasements, and groveling.

I, the Universe, the sun, the moon and the stars, the Alpha and the Omega, and all the rest, have created a paradise in time and space so that I, through you, might experience its infinite splendors, drink from its every cup, and live, love and be merry, in ways impossible without you.

Your desires, are my desires for you. What you want and when you want it, these were my ideas, too. Your dreams, are my dreams. You are the end all and be all of time and space, the only reason for this garden of Eden. You can do no wrong, there are no mistakes, and it's all good.

Follow your heart, delight in your preferences. Approve of yourself. Stake your claim, demand it, and hold out your hands. Banish your doubts, get off of your knees, and live as you please. Because, dearest, you can, and this is all I ever wanted.

With unspeakable love, I am,

The Universe

PS - ROAAAAAAAAAAAAAAR!

# Everything matters.

# Jambo! Universe here...

Golly, mid-year already, and boy,
do I ever need a vacation.

Can you imagine, having the entire world spin in the palm of your hand? Writing the script to history? Being able to change the course of eternity, by just changing your mind? Kind of far out, isn't it? But it's all right here in the brochure. Read it myself, "Spell binding! Intoxicating! The ultimate escape! Join billions on an unforgettable adventure into the jungles of time and space, to a "paradise found", where you are master of your destiny, all things are possible, and your every thought changes everything. So real, you may even forget who you are!"

Perfect for me, bags are packed.

Be cool, (just brushing up on the lingo.)

The Universe

PS – Let's do lunch.

# It's not so much

about having faith in yourself. Way too hard.
Besides, you can wrestle that croc after you
move mountains.

For now, just have faith in me, in the magic, and in
the unseen, and it shall be done.

Tallyho,

The Universe

# Never underestimate
## the Universe.

# Here's a little trick

on how to change the scenery in your life,
radically, fantastically, and perhaps, forever.
(If that's what you really want).

Look the other way.

# Adventurers Global Advisory

"Staying the course" should not be confused
with clinging to a cursed "how".

# Oh, "it's" not working?

Well, do you know where you'd be right now, what your life would be like, if it wasn't working?

Not reading this, for one. About half as good looking as you now are, two. And perhaps wondering, in a strictly spiritual sense, who let the dogs out.

The Universe


PS - It is working. And it's getting easier. And you are getting better, and better, and better.

# Whatever

you'd like to know, you already know.

Be still.

# If you knew for certain

that very, very soon, all your dreams would be coming true, what would you do today to prepare the way? (Do it.)

How might you celebrate? (Do this, too.)

Who would you tell? (Write them a brief note, now, you don't have to mail it, yet.)

What thoughts of gratitude would you have? (Express them.)

And finally, who would you help "achieve", as you have achieved? (Help them.)

# Whosoever may torment you,

harass you, confound you, or upset you,
is a teacher.

Not because they're wise, but because you seek to
become so.

# It all goes by so fast,
### doesn't it?

One minute you're here, and the next you're gone.

So really, you've got nothing to lose, have you?
Nothing! You're gonna make it "home" anyway.
You're gonna be exalted, and it's gonna be so
glorious, happy and easy.

Then, after a careful life review, you're gonna slap
your hand on your celestial forehead, jump up and
down with uproarious laughter, and say, "Dang, my
thoughts did become the things and events of my
life. That little book was right. And as exalted as I
am here, I was there. And as easy as it is here, so
could it have been there! I wanna play again, I
wanna go back. This time I promise not to forget. I
promise I'll believe in my dreams and myself. I'll
never let go. I'll never give up. I'll keep the faith.
Really I will."

# Actually, it's pretty simple.

You have one real choice: To do your best, with what you have, from where you are.

Everything else is just stalling.

# It's not possible!

You cannot significantly change your life, for better or worse, by manipulating the material world. Not by working harder, not by studying longer, not by schmoozing, not by sweating, not by fasting, not by the hair of your chinny, chin, chin.

But change, great change, is inescapable, when you first begin manipulating the world of your thoughts, which weigh a whole lot less than material things anyway.

It's that simple.

*You are the reason*
the sun came up today.

Believe it.

# Don't wait for those feelings

of excitement, confidence and expectation that will come when your life suddenly takes off, because your life cannot suddenly take off until you first have those feelings of excitement, confidence and expectation.

(Heck, if you have to, just pretend. Make believe, fake it. Right now, get up, walk down the hall, smile, wave, wink, pump your fist, and exude all over the place!)

# Some Investment Advice
## From The Universe

Did you follow your hunches during the 90's in the stock market? Did you hear what I was telling you about huge yields in real estate? Did you "stumble" across those itty-bitty public companies with stock offerings that made penny investors millionaires?

Phew, I was slammed doling out golden opportunities to anyone I could reach. It became kind of a hobby, you know, to fill in the gaps of boredom that go along with being the Universe.

Truthfully though, you didn't miss a thing. Those fortunes were chicken feed compared to what I offer on a full time basis through my day job. Are you ready for real opportunity? Do you even have room for the returns? No, you don't. But that's a good problem.

Thought. That's right. Thought is the greatest vehicle of all time for burying one's self, family and friends in wealth and abundance - no matter what's going on with the economy.

Thoughts have their own economy, and now is a super great time to get in on the ground floor.

With my patented trade secrets, I can take any old invisible thought of yours and turn it into a mine of gold, a mountain of cash, a well of prosperity.

It's not too late! The best is yet to come. Invest in thought, follow your hunches, and live the life of your dreams.

Public disclosure: This offer is irrevocable. You're now an investor whether you know it or not. All of your thoughts will become things. No lawyers can help you. Save yourself, choose the good ones.

# No matter how great

the temptation... (I'm talking about the temptation you're feeling *right this very second*), no matter how great...

STOP seeing yourself as just human!

You are *pure energy*, with an infinite reach.

# What a minute!

What does being a better you have to do
with anything?

Nothing! You're already smarter, kinder, more
honest, insightful, and ambitious, even better
looking, than 99.99% of the people who now live
in abundance, health and harmony. True? You
know it is!

It's not about being a better you, nor even a more
deserving you. It's about knowing you're
already both.

# What will it take for you

to begin having fulltime faith that there does
indeed exist, a magical Universe that is, at this very
moment, conspiring on your behalf?

How about your ability to read my thoughts, right
now, by deciphering these little black squiggles on
this book's page?

How about the fact that right now, billions of
atoms and cells are busy whirling about,
while holding you together?

How about the fact that your heart has beat some
22 times, without your help, since you began
reading this page?

How about all the lucky coincidences and happy
accidents that have brought you friends who now
love you and adventures to thrill, with more of
both on the horizon?

How about the fact that the sun rose this morning,
so that you might have another day, in paradise?

Hul-lo?

# There's nothing you can ask for

that won't set the *entire* Universe in motion.

Nothing. Nothing. *Nothing.*

# Courageous is the soul

who adventures into time and space to learn of
their divinity. For while they cannot lose, they can
think they have, and the loss will seem intolerable.
And while they cannot fail, they can think they
have, and the pain will seem unbearable. And while
they cannot ever be less than they truly are -
powerful, eternal and loved - they can think they
are, and all hope will seem lost.

And therein lies their test. A test of percep-
tions; of what to focus on, of what to believe in, in
spite of appearances.

Courageous indeed... the pride of the Universe,
and I should know.

# Never compromise a dream.

Do what you must. The fears, beasts, and mountains before you are part of the plan; stepping stones to a promised land; to a time and place that is so much closer than you even suspect.

Don't let your eyes deceive, for even as you read these words, your ship swiftly approaches.

# Can you imagine

actually being embarrassed by the enormity of wealth and abundance you've acquired? By the peace and harmony that pervades your life? By the ease and simplicity of everything you do? Almost feeling the need to apologize to those in your life who have yet to awaken and harness the principles that are free to all?

Start.

# What if, this very moment,

you realized you were dreaming. Dreaming you were at home, at work, wherever you now are, and that you were reading this "Note". And in that dream you also realized that as real as it all seemed, there was also a greater reality from which you were dreaming, and a greater essence that is yourself. That you came from eternity and will return to eternity, and that, in truth, you are your dream weaver.

Then suddenly, it dawned on you, that you could not awaken from this dream, until you first *demonstrated* this revelation, by claiming responsibility for your every manifestation heretofore, and exercising dominion over all things.

Yeeeeehaaaaaaaaaaaaaaaaaaaa!

# Just like before....

it's gonna happen, when you least expect it, from where you least expect it, and how you least expect it. So forget about it. Except, of course, to remember that it's gonna happen.

# Have you ever wondered...

at how you might change, once some of your grandest dreams are realized?

About how you'd behave differently if you already had a fabulous house on the lake, or if you were suddenly surrounded by mobs of loving and adoring friends?

You'd saunter. Yep, when you walked outside your home, through the 'hood, grocery store, or office, you'd saunter. You'd even saunter inside your home.

So start sauntering. Get into it. And maybe start winking, too.

Not only will people notice your calm, your grace and your confidence, but so will I.

# Of all the people,

in all the world, not a single one them....
is more precious, loved and deserving,
than you.

# You are creation's

first and last chance... to be you. Just as you are today. That's all you have to be.

Bask. It's more than enough.

# It's always best

to assume that everyone either knows the truth,
or will know the truth, because they either do,
or they will.

# What if there really was

a Santa Claus, an Easter Bunny, or a God who picked and chose among those whose prayers He answered; who got to decide who was ready for what, and who judged those He would either save or damn?

I know, I know!

Everyone could spend the rest of their lives hoping, wishing, and asking, instead of doing, being, and having.

Tally-ho, ho, ho!

PS – Think we'll get any presents after that one?

# Yo! This is the Universe,

## and have I got great news!

I've just finished distributing the power ball earnings and have lots and lots of time and energy and abundance left over. (You wouldn't even believe how much if I told you.) Here's what I'm thinking:

How would you like more money, more time, and more friends? Yes?! Well that's exactly what I've been working on!

Now, here's what you can do. At some point today, or during the week, take out a pen and paper (or use your computer if you like) and write a letter to someone who lives far away. Someone you love and respect, and share the "news" with them. I want you to write this letter as if these dreams of yours have already transpired, and I want you to tell them the whole enchilada. Write down every detail. Share with them your astonishment, the ramifications, and describe your happiness so that they (and I) can feel your emotions. Then, save that letter for when you really need it.

Hokey? Absolutely! A powerful act of thought and faith that will affect the course of your life.

Yes! Yes! Yes! Yes! Yes! Yes! Yes!

The longer the letter, and the greater the details, the more powerful the affect.

Your humble servant,

# For all the reasons

that you might draw someone into your life...
one would never be, to find their faults.

# Always, do what you can.
Because once you at least do what you can, no
matter how seemingly insignificant,
everything changes.

# Don't just see the magic,
engage it! Challenge it! Dare it! Dream big, with every expectation that your dreams *will* manifest.

Demand that they come true! You're not beholden to life, *life is beholden to you. You* are its reason for being. *You* came first.

# Do you realize that everyone,

absolutely everyone on this planet, grumpy office workers, arguing children, fickle spouses, the "narrow minded", the extremists, all think they're doing their very best?

So, how do you get through to someone who thinks they're doing their very best?

How would someone get through to you?

# Have you been there?

To that place of quiet bliss, of knowing that you're doing enough, wishing for nothing except what already is, exactly as it is, seeing the blue in the sky like you've never seen it before, watching a butterfly as if it appeared just for you, feeling so light that you're sure you could float, understanding the trials and tribulations of days gone by, and being glad for every single one of them, feeling so wrapped up in the present, that you couldn't care less about tomorrow, knowing that you're provided for, that the manifestation of your dreams is inevitable, and that the Universe flat-out adores you, reveres you, and wants for nothing, except to see your smile and hear your laughter?

That's right, very good, dearest. You're there now.

# Adventurers All Points Bulletin

We interrupt your day, to remind you that time is fleeting. Seconds, minutes and hours are completely vanishing. Right now, here today, you are the spring chick of your tomorrows.

Cluck, baby.

Thank you.

# I need your help with this one.

Please, just for a second, hold out the palm of your hand, and give it a quick glance. Now, imagine a miniaturized version of a loved one carefully and comfortably resting in it. Feel waves of your love blanketing this precious being. Imagine seeing the life of this loved one playing out in your palm and feeling their every joy and sadness. Imagine reading his or her mind and wanting nothing for yourself, except to see their dreams come true.

Then, you smile radiantly, filled with pride and joy, knowing that they are always safe, always provided for, never alone, and inescapably destined to learn of these truths for themselves. You smile because you know that the day of the their awakening swiftly approaches, as does their own sublime joy and the manifestation of their boldest dreams.

OK, that should do it.

Now, can you also imagine, that "someone else", right this very moment, is smiling down at you, as you play out your life, in the palm of their hand?

Yours truly,

# If it's hard,
there's something you're missing.

# Let's play doctor,

I'll be the doctor.

"What's the matter, dear one?"

"Sometimes I don't feel good."

"Hmmm, let me take a look at you. Well, you look fine, sound fine, all your parts are working. Everything seems to be in order. Tell me, what kind of thoughts have you been thinking lately?"

"The usual. Trying not to let the turkeys get me down, keep my head above water, you know, stuff everyone thinks. Just wanting to get by, hold my own, survive."

"Ah-ha, just as I thought, you've been thinking like everyone else, so now you feel like everyone else, kind of "blah".

"Well, here's a little trick. Stop trying to make so much sense of things. Stop being so logical. Stop thinking that the future depends upon what has been, or even what appears "to be". The props of your life are just props, fictional. You're not at the mercy of the past, the present, or the future... logic, reason or rationales. You are a Being of Light for whom all things remain possible, and there are no caveats to this truth.

"Feel better? Good."

Dr. Universe, Rx #77

# Close? You are so close

it's actually painful for those who know.

Poor "things". With bated breath they're writhing in anticipation, rolling in the aisles, imploring you to stay the course. They can see what lies in the unseen, they know of the coincidences and accidents that are about to be un-sprung, and they know if you could see them too, you'd be unstoppable.

Whatever you do next, please, think of your fans.

# Your Attention Please...

Your Attention Please...
This... is the Universe.

Today I'll be recording your *every* thought and emotion, no matter how "good" or "bad", no matter how generous or stingy, and no matter how helpful or hurtful they may be. *And everything I record*... will be played back for you, as soon as possible, as some type of physical manifestation in time and space.

Thank you, that is all.

# For as long as you are capable
### of anger, there are lessons to learn.

# Adventurer Advisory
## Global Alert!

Do not trust facts!!!! While they appear to be logical and self-proving, they are, perhaps, at the root of every evil (if you believe in evil). Here are 2 safeguards that will help keep you out of trouble:

First, do not ever look to facts for answers.

Second, never plan your life around them.

Facts masquerade as reality, when in fact (yuck, yuck), they're little more than stubborn, group opinions. Bad "facts"!

Just ignore 'em, and they'll go away.

# Give.

# A little birdie

just came my way and mentioned a deep,
soulful desire of yours.

Heavens no, not that one!

She said that you'd be eternally grateful if, once
and for all, you never, ever had to worry
about money again.

Well, I couldn't resist. Wish granted! You never,
ever have to worry about money again.

Anything else? Anything at all?

The Universe

# You could never spend

all the abundance that's yours to spend. Your supply is truly limitless.

Of course, of course, you already know that. The size of your supply isn't the issue, finding it is. You know it's there, you know it's yours, and you know you deserve it. But how to get your hands on it? That's the challenge.

Ah-ha, "how". Did you just ask "how"? You did.

Oh dear, never ask how. Never think about how, let go of the how's. If you wonder about how, it means your consciousness is not dwelling in spirit, it means you're trying to manipulate matter, and it means you're gonna be searching for a long, long, long, long time.

Steer clear of the "how's", dear heart, and simply dwell on the end result.

Got it?

# The real reason you chose

to be here – your purpose and mission in life –

Was to simply *be* who you now are.

Good reason.

You want more, *and that's good,*
very good. More money, love, energy, laughter.

OK, here's the deal... just remember that these
"things" lie only a *thought* away... not a career
away, not a year away, not a lucky break away, not
a relationship away... just a thought away.

O.K.?

Now, please, *think those thoughts.*

# Do you have any idea,
## of why I love you so much?

It's because if you were not exactly as you now are, for everything you've been through, I would not be exactly as I now am. And there are no words that can express, just how much more I am, because you are, just as you now are.

Oh... Gives me the chills.

Wonder no more.

Your grateful comrade in adventure,

The Universe

# The trick with imagination,

is remembering to use it.

Visualize every day.

# Your wishes

are what the Universe wishes for you. Your thoughts steer the ship of your dreams. And no matter where you've "been", nor how challenging your circumstances, right here and now is all that matters.

You are forever. Invincible. A Being of Light on an adventure of the highest order: to have fun and be happy in a magical, infinite, loving reality that conspires tirelessly in your favor; where thoughts become things, dreams come true, and all things remain forever possible.

Any questions?

# The reason you're "here"

is *not* to be good, to be better, to be perfect, to get "stuff" done, to save the world, to save somebody, to prove something, or to be anything... other than yourself.

That's *all* you have to work on. That's all you can do. But by doing it... all those other things will happen anyway.

# It's time you learned the truth.

Actually, you should have been told long, long ago.

You see, there was kind of a mix-up.

Things like this are never easy. But, well, to be as direct as possible...

You're not human.

Of course, you probably just think I'm being cute, but the truth, is that you are not human. Not even a little. Not one speck.

Now, before you go all ape, realize, there's a bright side to everything, and in this case, it's blinding....

You no longer have to behave as one.


Tallyho,

The Universe

# Someone once said,

"No pain, no gain."
And so it became their reality.

Bummer, huh?

# Amazing, simply amazing!

Do you realize that today, you may or may not receive certain phone calls, compliments, emails, surprises, letters, or visitors? Do you realize that today, you may or may not receive word of good or bad news? Do you realize that today, you may or may not encounter certain challenges, or triumphs, problems or victories?

And to think, you're the one who decides.

Wow.

Be good to yourself.

# If they're in your life,
## love them.

# When you understand someone,

*truly understand* someone, no matter who they are, you *cannot* help but love 'em, even though you might not always love what they do.

You knew that.

OK. Just as true, is that for anyone you feel less than love for, *no matter who they are,* it's because you do not truly understand them.

(No, you don't have to like what they do either, nor are you "supposed" to stay with them. You get to decide those things.)

# Your supply is the Universe,
## and its ways are infinite.

# It's about that time!!

Every 7 decades or so, all the stars line up exactly, exactly, as they now have, and an intergalactic, pseudo-quasi, invisible golden aura permeates every living and non-living thing. This is especially true on Fridays and Saturdays during this alignment. Even more so during months with 31 days. It doesn't hurt either that the planet's biorhythms are as they now are, and that Venus is rising on Mars. And, shhhhh, don't tell your fellow adventurers, but it's triple true for those with the same birthday as you!! What a coincidence, eh? Don't faint.

What might happen in the next 48 hours is anyone's guess.

During this time, the love that is always present here, becomes visible as this gold, making healings and manifestations really easy. Given your unique disposition, just by squinting you could probably see it. Go ahead.

From about the moment you read this email, for however long afterwards the alignment holds, your thoughts will begin working some unbelievable magic. Everyone you think of will feel them. No nook or cranny on the planet will be out of your reach, and the circumstances and events of your immediate future will become extraordinarily malleable.

Hint: Visualize now. Hurry!!

The last time this happened, email hadn't been invented, so no one even knew! Lucky for you, this is an awesome time to be alive.

Well, since you haven't started visualizing yet, I better 'fess up. I know what you're thinking, and you're right, the 7 decade stuff was bull. So was the star alignment thingy, but it wasn't *all* lies. You see, it's like people don't want to believe it's all so easy, so I thought if I made it trickier, I'd win more over.

It's tough being the Universe, so few want to believe in their utter and total dominion over all things. But I'll keep trying.

Have a golden weekend,

Tallyho,

PS - Did I make you squint?! Now, to make you believe the world spins in the palm of your hand.

# Do not think

that you have to get "there", wherever "there" is
for you, with what you have today, whether in
terms of money, confidence, talent, connections,
whatever. Doesn't work like that. Too scary.
Bad idea.

Once you set yourself in motion, the necessary
resources, in terms of money, confidence, talent,
connections, will be drawn to you.

{soft whisper in the background,
"Once you set yourself in motion..."}

Fade out.

# Here's a little workshop
on how to manifest absolutely anything...

1 - "Ask" once.

2 - Give thanks often.

End of workshop.

# What if it was true

that you make *your own* reality, and that your thoughts became the things and events of your life?

What would you do differently in the next 5 minutes? In the next 5 days?

# Time out! Time out!

What do you mean, it doesn't seem like it's working? You can't see your life turning around? It's hard? Ack!

Of course it doesn't seem like that, of course it seems hard! This is an adventure, you're an adventurer, and uncertainty and setbacks "happen". Besides, "easy" has never been your style, and setbacks are only ever stepping-stones to grander places.

The day your ship arrives, and it now swiftly approaches, the journey and the setbacks will be among your fondest memories.

Stay the course!

Resume play,

The Universe

PS - Challenges? Problems? Big deal!

# It does little good to say

you want something, and then, "just in case", prepare to do without.

Burn your bridges.

# Did you realize,

that whenever you gave anything, to anyone, you gave to the entire world?

And did you realize, that for every path you've walked, for every stone you've turned over, and for every door you've knocked on, you did so for everyone?

And finally, did you realize, that whenever you felt love, for any reason whatsoever, you irrevocably lifted the entire planet higher into the light?

Thanks, from all of us,

You rock!

# Logic is overrated.
## Big time.

There's always a way.

# Do you know what happens

just before something really incredible takes place?
Something mind blowing? Just before a really huge
dream comes true?

Do you?

Nothing.

Nothing happens. At least not in the
physical world.

So if, perchance, right now, it appears that
absolutely nothing is happening in your life...
consider it a sign.

Expect to be surprised.

# This is the Universe,
## and it's Friday!

As part of this week's Friday celebrations, I'm going to share a little secret with you. Actually, I should have shared it with you a few thousand Fridays ago, but most "people" aren't ready for this kind of secret. I've decided you're different.

It's the secret to getting anything, absolutely anything you want. OK? To magnetizing into your life, the things, emotions, and circumstances you dream of. All right? It explains how masters become masters, and adepts become adepts. And it'll finally convince you that I am always there with you to lend a hand, or perform a miracle. Cool?

Practice.

Yeah, practice. Because, just a little practice, goes farther than you could ever imagine.

PS- Now, fight the temptation to nod and shrug it off. Do something! Visualize just a little. Act with faith just a little. Explore your beliefs just a little. Manifest a little something; a phone call, a compliment, a flower, whatever. Expect a little miracle. Expect a little help. Expect it to be easy.

Practice.

# All roads lead to truth,
though some will take you there a whole heck of a
lot quicker than others.

Be honest with yourself.

# The Universe knows how.

# Adventurers All Points Bulletin

Have you discovered yet how some angels, like the ones who heal with their smile, who help light the way for others, and in whose path the flowers sway, are actually disguised as people?

And have you also noticed that some of them, don't even know they're angels?

Psssssst, looked into a mirror lately?

# What if there was only you,

and the rest of the world was "make believe",
imagination? If even the people in your life were
drawn there, or faded away, based upon
your thoughts.

Would it then be easier for you to grasp the true
meaning of limitless? Would you then believe, that
you alone make your reality?

Dearest, the rest of the world, is "make believe",
imagination. And all the people in your life are
there, or fade away, based upon your thoughts.

WOW... that was easy.

Tallyho, Limitless.

# Don't let those

who aren't in tune with you,
distract you from those who are.

# How much longer

before you revel in the awareness that you are enough, that you've done enough, and that you're now worthy of your heart's greatest desires?

What has to happen for you to give this to yourself?

No biggie. Just wondering. Take your time.

# You chose your dreams

for the journeys they'd inspire, and you knew when you chose them that there'd be obstacles, dark days, and knuckleheads who'd stand in your way. They're part and parcel of where you're headed, and they don't just go away.

So when you face your next challenge, welcome it. Rise up, don't back down. See it as a stepping-stone, not a wall; a valley, not an abyss. And before you know it, as one is conquered after another, the journey will be complete, and the joy of manifesting your dream will pale in comparison to the satisfaction of your persevering, overcoming, and breaking through.

Don't you see, these are the days, *right now*, mid-adventure, that will mean the most to you, once your dreams come true?

Enjoy.

# Isn't it curious

how people pick others to be in their lives, at
work, at home, and to play, not because they're
perfect, but to have fun, learn and grow? But then,
shortly after they arrive, they're often unhappy
because those they picked aren't perfect?

What am I missing?

# No one in your shoes

could have done better than you've done, with where you began, what you had, and all you've been through. No one.

Aren't you glad it wasn't easier?

# Can you imagine the joy,

the peace, the complete sense of satisfaction? The harmony, the love, and stitches of laughter? Can you imagine the interest income?!

Good, because nothing else shapes mountains, people and bank accounts, quite like imagination.

Ka-Ching.

# It's the thirst for approval,

validation and justification, from sources outside of yourself, that blinds you to the fact that they need not be earned.

# Let's pretend, just for today,

all day long, throughout our every thought and
decision, that life is easy, that everyone means
well, and that time is on our side. OK?

And let's pretend that we are loved beyond belief,
that magic conspires on our behalf, and that
nothing can ever hurt us without our consent.
All right?

And if we like this game, we'll play tomorrow as
well, and the next day, and the next, and pretty
soon, it won't be a game at all, because life, for us,
will become those things. Just as it's become what
it is, today.

Thoughts become realities, too.

# Adventurers All Points Warning

Today, you will be challenged. Challenged, by the grand illusion. Tempted to look to time, space and all things material, for understanding; to judge your place in the world; and to make decisions about your life.

Fight it.

Go within.

Remember the magic.

Be vigilant.

# Imagine watching TV

and you see a German Shepard at the beach with a tennis ball in it's mouth. Suddenly, with a subtle flick of its head, the dog throws the ball, with pinpoint accuracy, to it's master 100 feet away. Or, you watch a program where you see a Ferrari traveling at 160 mph, headed straight for a group of people standing in the middle of the road, eating shrimp and caviar, and at the precise point necessary, the car rapidly decelerates, abruptly stopping less than a single millimeter before disaster, and no one flinches.

What kind of TV do you watch anyway?

Your brain wants to say, "no way", because it wants logic and the physical senses to interpret reality, but the cinematographers have you in the palm of their hand, unbound by rules, free to play films in reverse, without telling you.

The Universe is the same, its trump card lies in orchestrating an unseen reality that escapes both logic and physical senses.

It's as if the Universe works backwards, too. You think of the end result, what you want to happen in your life, and then the Universe works backwards, aligning your dreamed-of life with where you are today, stringing together people, places, and events, for the "impossible" to become possible.

This *is* how life works.

Trust the Universe, it knows how. Don't tie its hands with logic, fear, or limiting beliefs. And next year the Oscar for trick photography... could be yours.

# What if, all the people
in your life, every single one of them, even the
pesky ones, asked to be there, so that your light
might brighten their way?

# It's so tempting

to look at your present life situation, at who
you're with, to where you work, to what you have
and have not, and think to yourself, "This was
obviously meant to be, I'm here for a reason." And
to a degree, you'd be right. But you are where you
are because of the thoughts you used to (and may
still) think, and so you are where you are, to learn
that this is how life works – NOT because it was
meant to be.

Don't give away your power to vague or
mysterious logic. Tomorrow is a blank slate in
terms of people, work, and play, though because it,
too, will be of your making, you will again have
that sense that it was meant to be, no matter who
or what you've drawn into your life.

Nothing is meant to be, except for your freedom
to choose and your power to create.

Choose big and be happy.

# Do you think the Universe

ultimately rewards those who live in poverty? Do you think those who toil and sweat from paycheck to paycheck, are more likely to inherit the Kingdom than those who work in ivory towers? Does the Universe take special notice of sacrifices? Is it pleased when some put the needs of others before their own? Does the Universe favor those who strive to live spiritual lives?

Actually, honey, the Universe doesn't give a flying yahoo. It loves you no matter what rules you make up.

Talk about unconditional.

It's *your degree of faith,*
your belief in benevolent powers and events
*unseen,* that summons *the magic,* either in huge
gobs, or in drips and drops.

Go for gobs, it costs the same.

# Visualizing for Beginners...
for those who want convenient parking spaces,
unexpected gifts, or chance encounters with
cool people:

First, think. Second, let go.


# Visualizing for the Illuminated...
for those who want a healing touch, world peace,
or a new Bentley Azure:

First, think. Second, let go.


Choose carefully.

# Dues?

Those were all taken care of eons ago! You don't
have any more dues to pay!

I know, I know, you don't believe it.

OK, Plan B. You do have dues to pay. You must
slave and scrimp, wriggle and pimp, work
overtime, pound the pavement, sacrifice, barter,
and be selfless. Endure the stupidity of others,
work a job you don't love, and unlearn a lifetime of
bogus teachings.

Are these the dues you believe in? Well then,
haven't you paid these too, ten times over?

# It's as if you won

the Universe's "Live The Absolute Life Of Your Dreams" lottery, a long, long, long time ago. But instead of finally checking your ticket... you keep on buying more... hoping, wishing and praying.

# Think of everyone
on the planet, everyone, as your special friend...

And so they shall become.

Dang.

# Do you think
that the Universe longs to
"Give you the Kingdom"?

Well, it doesn't.

You see, your Highness, that transaction took
place absolutely ages ago.

Tallyho,

# Just a reminder

in case you forgot, in case you've thought otherwise, or in case you never knew...

There is nothing you can't have.

There is nothing you can't do.

There is nothing you can't be.

OK?

# Whoa! Happy days! Rock on!

I just read about you in the Universal Times! *The Universal Times!* Sure enough, there you were, picture and all "...this exemplary Being of Light, residing on planet Earth, in their year 2003 - I said to myself, "I know that Being of Light!!" - has been awarded the *Double-Secret Medal of Honor* for bravery and valor in seeing through the illusions of time and space!"

Now, this is no little thing! It's huge! Because even while "Time~Space" is a primitive school, it's still the most hypnotic adventure ever dreamed up. In fact, only the most courageous are even allowed to participate. And of these, only a teensy, tiny percentage ever come to realize that it's all illusions; that they craft their own destinies; and that in spite of all physical appearances to the contrary, any life can turn around on a dime. Fewer still, receive the *Double-Secret Award!*

My word, you are extraordinary, and it's about time you received the recognition you deserve. But, there's a reason it's "double-secret". If you share this news with lesser mortals... Let's not go there. Shhhhhh.

Tallyho,

PS - You looked smashing in white, but what's with the hat and feathers?

PPS - Now, remember why you won.

# What good does it do

knowing approximately where the treasure lies, yet never digging? Having a bank account with millions in it, but never writing a check. Or discovering the fountain of youth, but never drinking a drop?

You must live the truths you discover, you must break your old rules, defy logic, *be* the change. Dig, write the check, and drink eternally, one little step after another.

I'm sorry, but there's no other way.

Tallyho,

PS - Of course, you can ask for help.

# Question: What would it take,

what would have to happen in your life these days,
for you to allow yourself to really kick back, relax
and just enjoy?

Answer: Whatever it is, *whatever*, you will achieve
it, earn it, acquire it, or experience it *so much
faster*, if you first, kick back, relax and just enjoy.

Simple enough?

# Good news!

By virtue of your brave presence in time and space, an often challenging and sometimes even frightful arena, you're pre-qualified for platinum Universal assistance.

This coverage is unlike any other on the market. As a Time~Space Adventurer, you have at your disposal our unlimited resources, invisible principles, and trillions of years of experience, momentum, and overhead.

We can solve any problem, intervene in any crisis and, quite effortlessly, shock and delight the senses at a moment's notice. And best of all, this coverage is free, eternal, and irrevocable. In fact, even if you wanted to, you couldn't leave home without it.

In order to activate your coverage, simply give thanks. Thanks in advance that the help you stand in need of has already been provided.

Please, be our guest, enjoy these privileges that you so richly deserve.

# Here's the thing.
It - whatever "it" is for you,
relationships, money, life - will never, *ever*, be
easy... until you first begin thinking of "it" as easy.

Chic-a-boom,

The Universe

# You see, it's the same

with everything. It must happen in thought first. It must. Even when, especially when, by all outer appearances, your desires seem preposterous.

Anyone can think happy thoughts when they're happy, wealthy thoughts when they're wealthy, healthy thoughts when they're healthy.

Your life's mission was to create the stage you're now on so that you'd have reason to awaken from your slumber. To have dreams worth pursuing and the passion to press on, in spite of the conditions surrounding you. To learn you must look beyond your illusions, and to grasp that your dreams, are indeed, what's meant to be.

This is the Holy Grail. Your search is over. Go out on a limb, give it your unending best, and never, ever, ever give up. There haven't been any accidents, you haven't made any mistakes, and the perfection is excruciating - you'll see.

Carry on brave heart,

# What if, what if suddenly,

in a flash of fire and light, you got it! And among other things, you suddenly understood, without a doubt, the creative power of your word. Do you think you'd ever again utter, "it's hard", "it's not working", "something's wrong with me", or "I don't know"?

Nope, you wouldn't, not ever again.

# "Ohhhhh my...

oh my Gooooood!

"No way! Unbelieeeevable!!!!!!!

"I'm freakin'... Totally freakin'... Get out of here!

"Oh no, no, no! Please, don't let this be a dream.

"Eiy-yie-yie...

"Can you believe it's me? I can't. Guess I can.
Guess I did! Yeah me!

"U-ga-chuga, U-ga-chuga, (uhmpf!)
I can't help this feeling...

"Better than even *I* had imagined. Way.

"Thank you, Universe!"

Very nice. Very nice, indeed. Great visuals, super expressions, careful not to over do it with the hip swivel on "uhmpf".

That's all the practicing we'll have to do today, won't be long now. Won't be long at all.

# Do you know why you are you?

Because no one else could be.

# *Of course* there are "things" you
## want that you don't yet have!
## They're why you're here.

# Do you realize that for any

dream of yours to come true, the dreams of others take huge leaps forward? Not just indirectly, but directly. People like partners, family members, your agent, your reps, your suppliers, your custom homebuilder, your publisher, and so many more. Even people you don't yet know. Then, as their dreams advance, the dreams of their associates are advanced, and then their associates, and then theirs, and so on, and so on.

What's really cool, is that way deep down, they all know this, ahead of time, and, they all know you. In fact, whenever you dream, and move with those dreams, those among the masses whose own dreams are aligned with and compliment yours, are psychically summoned. Pacts are formed, deals are made, and coincidences calculated. Odds increase exponentially, and risks are minimized (if you believe in odds and risks). And you are propelled even further and faster by their energy as well as your own.

In fact, I was actually asked to write this "Note" to you on behalf of all those whose lives will be dramatically enhanced by your dreams coming true. Your team, as it were.

# Today, treat everyone,

exactly the way you would treat them, *as if* you
had already "arrived", because behind their eyes,
the Universe is watching, looking for direction, as
it paints each moment of time.

Do DO Do Doo Do DO Do Doo...

# Embrace criticism,

whether from the wise, or from fools. Never has a
word been uttered that didn't have meaning, to
those who heard it.

# Anger closes the mind,
### and cools the heart, at a time when both are needed most.

# Hubba, Hubba, Hubba.

Ya' know how the bud of a flower looks? Already attractive, special and unique, yet still barely hinting at the splendor and magnificence to come. Oblivious itself, of how its presence will add to the world.

That's what you remind me of.

The Universe

# That's right. This is a dream.

You're still asleep. Any minute now, an elephant might appear behind you, wearing a pink tutu and tennis shoes. Or maybe the phone will ring, and it'll be Abraham Lincoln to ask why you're late for the ball. Or perhaps, Oprah is down the hall, live audience in tow, about to introduce you as her new favorite author. Anything can happen in a dream, *anything*, without regard to the past, without regard to logic, and you never have to figure out the "how's".

Learn from your dreams, because the stuff of time and space is no different. Forget your past. Pitch the logic. And drop the cursed how's.

Tallyho,


PS - Cute whiskers.

# Can you imagine having

made a difference in so many lives that people, everywhere, talk about you for the rest of their lives? Can you imagine truly leaving the world a better place than you found it? Can you imagine that all the angels might know your name?

You have. It's done. They do.

Good God almighty, what are you gonna do next?

Just one of your many fans,

The Universe

PS - And you're so young!

# You, yes you holding this book,

are the one who was sent to make a difference, to be a bridge, to light the way, by living the truths that have been revealed to you, so that others might do the same.

Now do you know why you've always seen the world so much more clearly than others?

To help.

# This is the Universe,
and have I got some "goodish" news for you
(the "ish" isn't so good)!

The good news - you know the stuff you want -
wealth and abundance, friends and laughter - I
think you once said, a fabulous house on the lake?
Well it's all done... hurray!

Your burning desires, the intense yearnings you've
felt, the highly pitched longing, and your silent
pining for these things and more, have actually
created this world... in another dimension.
(That's part of the "ish".)

In fact, I can see a "probable" you there now,
lolling about in the lap of luxury, giggling and then
roaring with laughter, doing the "lawn mower",
"high-fiving" your friends, and them all turning
various shades of green with envy. You know,
you're a real hoot when you're so happy.

But there's more "ish". Seems the yearning and
pining, have actually distanced you from this reality
you've created. You see, thoughts of "I want, I
want, oh God, how I want" are picked up by the
Universe, me, as "I don't have, I don't have, oh

God, how I don't have", and then these thoughts manifest, as all thoughts do, perpetuating the lack!

To remove the "ish", here's the dish: Start with the "thank you, thank you, oh God, thank you", and behave accordingly.

Mow on maestro,

# And sometimes, you wonder

whether or not you've been realistic, whether or not it's within you, whether or not "it" really works. But in your wondering, you've given pause to an entire Universe that never once thought to doubt, and yet still, is poised, to deliver.

# Pop Quiz

Q: How do you find love, health, abundance, or enlightenment?

A: Stop searching. And start seeing what's been there all along.

# There are no tough times,
hard knocks, or challenges that aren't laden with
emeralds, rubies and diamonds, for those who see
them through.

# Isn't it a hoot?

Of all the people in all the world who actually "get it", few, if any, actually give it to themselves.

The trick? Baby steps.

Give, just a little, today. Give credit, give praise, give goodies, to yourself, and the Universe will give you even more.

Selfishness *is* a virtue, unless *you think* it must come at the expense of others. And why would anyone think that? Oh yeah, that's what all the people who don't "get it" told you.

You *are* ready.

# The secret to getting rich
is knowing that you already are, *and acting like it.*

PS - Darling, do tell me who manages your assets. And those gems! Are they real?

(Answer: The Universe, and real what?)

# All you have to do,
is *be*. Be yourself.

There's nothing to prove. And there's no one to
please who isn't already over the moon with joy at
how well you've done, and with who
you've become.

# Uh-oh...

Good news and bad news again.

First, the bad news. In the days, weeks, and months ahead, you're very likely gonna have the same dang problem that you have today.

Now the good news. The only real problem you have today, is thinking that you have problems.

You just don't.

The Universe

# Someone so cool,

something so neat, and somewhere so wonderful,
are all on the menu. You just have to make up
your mind and order.

And you should see dessert...

# You must use what you've got.

Talent, brains, heart. Instincts, hunches, feelings.
Money, health, friendships. Time, space, stuff.

Otherwise, why would more be given?

You rock,

# Limits are for those
who don't believe in the Universe.

# Knock, knock. _____ _____?

It's me, the Universe, and I've heard a little rumor.

Seems someone on earth is asking for their own fabulous home in the country!!!! Phew, wouldn't that be nice! Know anyone?

I thought so. Well guess what?

I have one, and it's ready for delivery!

Would you do me a little favor?

Would you tell them that in order to get it from here to there, all they have to do is close their eyes, count to three, click their heels, give thanks that it's already in their life, and begin moving towards it?

No, no. Some of that's "make believe", but so is their fabulous home in the country, until they stop asking, and start giving thanks and moving towards it.

Tallyho,

PS - Do something.

# Can you feel
your heart beating?
It's beating in 3's today.
Go on, right now, feel it.

It's saying, "I~^ love~^ you~^!"
And it really does.

# Understanding...
## is the elixir of life.

# If you could see, just how life

was meant to be... you'd probably faint.

Because things would look exactly like they look today, and you'd find that *you* are exactly where you're "supposed" to be, in an adventure without end.

# It's OK to love material things;
matter is *pure spirit.*

# And on Friday, the Universe said,
## "Yo! Ho! Ho! It's time to have fun!"

Whereupon it invented imagination, and there was a huge gasp among the angels. For it was clear that the reins of power in time and space had been passed to those so blessed, and that they would be left to discover this for themselves.

And it was good.

Happy anniversary!

PS - And as the angels quickly gathered, there, in line, stood you.

# Your Attention Please...

Your Attention Please.

This, is the Universe.

Would whoever gave thanks for a home on the lake, more friends, and a couple of million bucks, please specify which lake, what kind of friends, and provide some kind of general time frame?

Hul-lo?

Details. If they don't know, how can I?

# You've been worthy.

## You are worthy. You'll be worthy.

# Of course,

"Here & Now" is what *really* matters, but people will be people, so.... given that you're a FOREVER BEING, I do hope you're spending as much time looking forward, as you are looking back.

Because really, forever means you have quite a lot to look forward to.

# Here's a snippet of advice
that comes from an as yet undiscovered
manuscript buried deep in some Pyrenees
mountain cave...

"Choose feelings over logic, adventure over
perfection, here over there, now over then, and
always, love, love, love."

It also said "you rock", but you never
would have believed that.

# If the Universe suddenly

appeared before you in the form of a wise, old,
kindly messiah with a glowing white aura, and
presented you with a one hundred point game plan
that would guarantee, *guarantee,* your dreams
coming true, but first required that you let go of all
your worldly possessions, shave your head, walk
on a bed of nails, sacrifice 3 hours every day
training your mind, and invest a minimum of 2
years before you began to see the first changes.
Would you follow the plan? Would you follow it *if
all of your dreams would then come true?*

Did you say yes? I know you said yes.

Now, if the Universe suddenly appeared before
you on the pages of this book, spoke to your
heart, and said that in order to begin living the life
of your dreams within 1 year, or less, all you had
to do was imagine the life of your dreams
(visualize 5 minutes a day), move with the life of
your dreams (with a token act of faith performed
just once a day), and honestly face your fears,
would you even try?

Hmmmm...

If visualizing were extremely difficult, maybe then
people would do it. Oh yeah, they'd form clubs,
give designations, have car washes!

# If time and space are illusions...

doesn't that mean you come "from", and now exist in, a "place" that "precedes" both?

Wouldn't this then mean that you're really everywhere, always?

It does, and you are...
UNLIMITED beyond your wildest imaginings.

# You wouldn't believe
the stuff people think they want.

Just the other day someone was asking for a llama.

Nothing wrong with llamas, I have a few myself,
but the llama he wants is supposed to help him
with his business; schlepping stuff over mountains,
they're good for that.

Now, why do you suppose he
didn't just ask for a pickup truck?

Trust me, he could've asked for a pickup truck,
and he'd have been a lot happier.

So... I'm off to the bazaar. In the meantime, should
*you* need anything, please, *be sure to ask for what
you really want.*

# The good thing,
about bad things, is that they make way for even better things.

# Agh aghmmm... it's me again...
the Universe.

I'm feeling kind of adventurous today. You?

Tell you what... let's do away with some rules.
Gravity for starters. Time too. Let's fly and be
young again. Younger, I mean. Like kids.

Close your eyes and meet me over the very
building you're now in... hovering in space, looking
down at its roof, and off into the horizon that
surrounds us. Imagine this as I go...

We're slowly gazing all around, and soaking up the
beauty that's everywhere. When suddenly, in a
flash, everything's turned snowy white. Pure,
radiant white, above, below, and everywhere we
look. Nothing visible but white, with one,
microscopic exception. In the distance,
unimaginably far, far away, we see what looks like
a tiny, tiny, tiny speck... of gold.

Ummmmmm... Gold is always good.

At first it appears that the gold is slowly, really
slowly, getting bigger. But what's actually
happening is that we're getting closer to it. At first

it seems we're moving slowly, but actually, we're moving at the speed of light - then even faster. It's just that the gold is so, so far away.

Ages pass, but the ride is awesome! Galaxies pass, but it's sooooo exciting! Light years pass, but time stands still.

Now... there's no more white. Just gold. Nowhere to go, because we're already there. And it turns out, this gold is so much more than a color because you can hear it too, kind of purring. And you can feel its luxurious warmth on your skin, all over your body, and as you breath it, the aroma's like roses, or plumeria, or jasmine.

Most peculiar is that you sense it's alive, supremely intelligent and acutely aware... of you. You know it knows what you're thinking, what you're feeling, and it's as if your happiness is all that it cares about.

Not just alive, but responsive too, impressionable, obliged even, to flood your physical senses with all that you can imagine, as it's about to do.

Suddenly, the gold begins sparkling. Billions and billions of sparkles envelop you... flashing, winking, shining... And slowly, slowly, slowly it begins to fade away… Pixel for pixel, sparkle for sparkle, it begins manifesting itself into something even more spectacular, dazzling, and magical than what it was…

Lo and behold, before your very eyes, right this very moment, the gold has transformed itself into… *today*. Yet another day in paradise.

Wow. Welcome back.

By the way, the gold was me all along. So is today. And I love you with all of my heart.

Tallyho,

The Universe

xxoo

PS – I had to turn the gravity back on… but you're still younger.

PPS – Whenever you want a change of scenery, just summon the gold.

# If you only knew

just how literally true *all* of these "Notes" are - concerning your power, your strength, and your divinity, about the love, the magic, and the infinite possibilities - for the next few days, you'd see the rest of the world... through tears.

And you'd never stop giving thanks.

Ain't life grand?

# Help spread the word!

A selection of these "Notes" are freely available as
e*cards on the Internet at www.tut.com

# TUT® Adventurers' Club Oath

"In the face of adversity, uncertainty and conflicting sensory information, I hereby pledge to remain ever mindful of the magical, infinite, loving reality I live in. A reality that conspires tirelessly in my favor. I further recognize, that living within space and time, as a Creation amongst my Creations, is the ultimate Adventure, because thoughts become things, dreams come true, and all things remain forever possible. As a Being of Light, I hereby resolve to live, love and be happy, at all costs, no matter what, with reverence and kindness for All.
So be it!"

*Take the Oath online, at www.tut.com, and begin receiving your FREE, personalized, daily, never-before-published, "Notes from the Universe" via email!*

*Jambo Fellow Adventurer!*

If someone told you the truth about life, reality, and the powers you possessed, would you recognize it as the truth? **If someone offered you keys to the kingdom of your wildest dreams, would you accept them?** It might not be so easy, given our immersion in a society that tells us, reminds us, and insists, that we're limited, aging "creatures", who live lives between luck and fate, in a hard, unforgiving world. But the truth, and this will likely ring bells in your heart of hearts, is that we are **INFINITE and POWERFUL, fun loving gladiators of the Universe; Adventurers just being human, with eternity before us,** *and the power of our thoughts to help shape it.*

There could be no better time than now, at this crossroads in history, to discover the truth about who you are, and all that you can be, which is the purpose behind **"Infinite Possibilities: The Art of Living Your Dreams"**. It's an audio program aimed at the "Truths of Being"; becoming aware of them, understanding them, and harnessing them. My mission throughout is to remind you of:

- **How POWERFUL you are,**
- **How FAR you can reach, and**
- **How much you DESERVE,**

so that you can begin thriving as the giant you are, in a kingdom where you have indeed been given dominion over all things.

**Blood, sweat and tears ARE NOT what it takes to see your dreams come true. Imagination, belief**

**and expectation are what's needed.** Then you're drawn into action, circumstances and "coincidences" that make dream manifestation INEVITABLE. This isn't wishful thinking; it's the way things have always been in time and space.

You don't need more education, connections, or lucky breaks, **you just need to understand the principles and concepts that every prophet and messiah has shared since the beginning of time.** Principles that have nothing to do with religion, but everything to do with the truth about who you are, why you're here, and the magic at your disposal.

There is nothing you can't do, nothing you can't have, and nothing you can't be.

- **You do have the power,**
- **You are guided, and**
- **The Universe IS conspiring on your behalf!**

You've chosen an exciting time to be alive. At the dawn of our civilization's awakening to truth. Especially exciting for pioneers like yourself, who've come with **an instinctive understanding of how life really works,** and who've risen to the task of being among the first to test the truths they know, living the life of their dreams *because they can*, and helping to light the way for others.

That you've read this far is no accident. *Please join me*, Adventurer to Adventurer, so that you, too, can **discover how effortless the art of living your dreams was meant to be**.

Your great admirer,

**www.tut.com**

# TOTALLY UNIQUE THOUGHTS®

**...because thoughts become things!®**

Launched in 1989 by 2 brothers and their cool mom, TUT® believes that everyone's special, that every life is meaningful, and that we're all here to learn that dreams really do come true.

We also believe that "thoughts become things®", and that imagination is the gift that can bring love, health, abundance and happiness into our lives.

Totally Unique Thoughts®
TUT® Enterprises, Inc.
Orlando, Florida
www.tut.com
USA